F*d-Up Poetry
for
F*d-Up People
in
F*d-Up Times

Collection of Poems
1993 - 2021

Shwa Laytart

Avantpop Publishing
Las Vegas, Nevada
2025

PREFACE

Like many poets, I started writing to woo the ladies. The next obvious step was then to write about heartbreak. Without a doubt, love and heartbreak are the stepping stones each poet crosses along their journey as a writer. To speak of a person's beauty in every way possible and how their majesty is above all else is the foolish sauce that pours from a young artist's pen. Only to be replaced with the gut-wrenching lava that seeps onto the paper, devouring all beauty, once that adolescent love has been demolished and turned to dust. I was thirteen when I wrote my first love poem, and thirteen when I wrote my first heartbreak poem.

Growing up, music was a major part of my life. I wrote my first lyrics when I was seven and my parents had just divorced. A simple song about birds and wishing I were one and could just fly away. I never wrote it down, I just sang it to myself when I was alone. Aside from musicians and lyricists, there were only two poets in my life. Theodor Geisel and Shel Silverstein. Best known for their children's books. Books that I reread hundreds, if not thousands of times. As a child who struggled with dyslexia, the word-play and twisted rhymes both writers used have always been comforting to me. To this day, these two poets are still my favorites.

In high school, my poetry often made it into the school paper. It wasn't long after that when girls started asking me to write poems for them which was easy for me, because I was in love with each and every one. This, however, did create serious issues with their boyfriends, but that's for another story. Once my poetry began to get noticed, it wasn't long before the critics began to attack. From time to time my social and political views were judged, but mostly, it was my writing style that was the main issue. Not only did my writing peers tell me I was doing it wrong, but so did a few teachers. You see, the "issue" is that my poetry style of writing is rhyming. Rhyming was considered "the style of amateurs. Not something someone with talent should be doing," an English teacher once told me. My writing peers were so displeased that my poems were making it into the school paper (and being loved by some) that they asked the paper to stop printing my work. What else was I to do? I took their advice and wrote dozens of poems that didn't rhyme. Eventually, the rhymes started to slip back into my work. First, a couple of lines. Then, a few verses, and before I knew it, rhyming was back in full force, from start to finish. I had come to realize that rhyming was the style that I loved, and I didn't see any issue with it. Even if it was wrong.

Over the years, my poetry has taken on more of a dark and satirical vibe. Writing about injustice, greed, the destruction of nature, abstract human nature, the surreal, the underground, and the daily comedy of errors. Someone at a book expo years ago called me the Dark Dr. Seuss.

A title I wear like a badge of honor. If it is the Dark Dr. Seuss or the Sarcastic Silverstein I am known as, then so be it. These were my childhood mentors, and I will continue the tradition of writing poetry that rhymes. In a recent poem from my new upcoming collection, I write:

Now, if you don't like poems that rhyme, then call it rap.
Like Jurassic 5 said, *I use my words like a Glock automatic.*

I love the poems I write, and for years, my poetry was just for me and the handful of people I shared it with. It wasn't until my wife decided to gather together some of our favorite poems that I've written, nearly 30 years in the making, and put them together as a book. In 2021, the first edition of F*D-UP POETRY for F*D-UP PEOPLE in F*D-UP TIMES was released. Since then, Avantpop Publishing has sold nearly a thousand copies. That's all thanks to those crazy readers of poetry who don't mind that I'm doing it wrong.

As my mentors once told me:

"Today you are you! That is truer than true! There is no one alive that is youer than you!"

"Be yourself and the people that don't mind are the people that matter."
- Dr. Seuss

"There are no happy endings. Endings are the saddest part. So just give me a happy middle and a very happy start."

"Although I cannot see your face as you flip these poems awhile....
Somewhere from some far-off place, I hear you laughing, and I smile."
- Shel Silverstein

I hope you too enjoy this second edition. I can promise you this: I will continue to do it wrong.

Shwa Laytart
September 6, 2025

TABLE OF CONTENTS

PARTY CONVERSATION

So check this out

We're traveling through space and time
Each year we progress further into the unknown
Yet we continue to repeat patterns
In nearly the exact same mosaic form
As they were previously performed

So check this out

We're all living and breathing
And experiencing the same thing
As we reincarnate each time
From death to life from life to death
Circling and circling
From best to worst
From worst to best

So check this out

If we take into consideration
All the mistakes that we make
And know that others
Will have that same fate
For I am you and you are me
So If I hurt you I'm also hurting me

So check this out

I turn to the person across the bar
And said *with this kind of knowledge*
I think we'd go far

They replied with a slurred confidence

Well it seems to me
You have no doubt
Your story is loopy
But sounds like you've
Figured
It
Out

THE STRUGGLE

I'm thinking too hard again
And I just lost my place

Mud-sliding axis
Silent
Release

Tea on the grass is of empirical need

Relocated Natives have no territorial rights
Most people I meet have no concept of time

I'm a violet cloud in a warm jet-stream
In a jar
In a box
On a shelf in the garage

When talking telepathically
Think gently before you speak
Guide that chakra energy

As common companions meet every day
Life fungus spore mushrooms after the rains

Drinking and driving the conversation
You know who your true friends are
when you don't have a car

THE FAMILY TREE
AIN'T NOTHING BUT HISTORY,
SO WHAT DO I TELL MY MOTHER?

We could drink every night
Slow cold forgiveness
Humbles long day fright

Drunken nights are doors
Into my daydreams
The only time I cry
Is in my sleep
Reality just ain't what it seems

My father was Jim Morrison and psilocybin
My mother was a Native American slave
In my last life, I was a pirate
Who went down with an ancient island
In this life, I'm a pilot
Who only comes down every other day

Jesus was an alien
Placed into a virgin
In a time of need
So where's the beginning of the conspiracy?

Broken car bones
Don't run anymore
Because slumbering
Burns off energy
So don't forget
Every soul is electricity

Along the backstreets in the morning
Families wait in cars
To visit the prisoners in the stockades

Do you still believe the foolish things
Your parents say?
Just because they believe
In God and traditional holidays?

How many orbits around the sun
Until the moth burns its wings?

Solitude in the next plan of attack
For a shrinking society

Living at the edge of a much larger universe
Dark is but a state of mind
We're all dinosaurs, laughed the monkey

I'll meet you at the sauna
To burn off this week's impurities
Forced daily detoxification
With psychic terrorism, you need vitamin B

Medicines made by poison chemical companies

Brainwashed at birth
Some stumble onto insight

When there's nothing else to eat
Make tasty meals
From dead animals on the roadside

If cards are played
To pass the time
Then the hand you were dealt
Is not unlike mine

It could be worse
Said a war surviving nurse
Your father could have been
An enemy soldier
Who raped your mother
And murdered your brothers
And taught you the true meaning of the word
Cancer

But in a hundred years
No one will care
Unless
You build a multinational corporation

So drink your wine
And spend the night
With your best friend
Your cat
Or a caring neighbor

Because as you can see
In these times
Not even a rooted tree
Can live
Half of forever

MONGRELS

So the story goes
My great grandmother
An old Mescalero Indian woman
With long gray hair and a love for cactus
Played with Geronimo when they were very young

There are many stories in my family
That cover a plethora of adventures, close calls,
And misfortunes
You see, I come from a long line
Of mixed race love affairs
The cultural melting pot that is the United States
Is my family pot-luck

Native-American-Mexican-Native-Mexican-American-
African-
American-South-American-Asian-American-Caucasian-
Half-Breeds

Our ethnicity being the lifestyle of love
And circumstance
And happenstance
Which
You can't determine this
By first glance

My cousin Raymond joined the army and said there
Everyone is just American
Nationally, I can accept that
And I guess being born there makes me a Californian

But deep down aren't we all just mixed-breeds?
Collectively, simply Earthlings?

Also have you noticed
Pure-breeds always have
The most disease?

My mutt family has many stories
Because our bloodline crosses
The global boundaries

So, much like my ancestors
I roam the streets
Driven by love
For any adventurous Earthling

DEAD CITY ROT

Dead City Rot
Dead City Rot
Take this fucking stupid story
You've told me
And flush it down your hollow trunk

Dead City Rot
I hope your limbs
All fall off
I hope the rain and the wind
Strip your rusty crust
Flesh

Can't make you see
Through blood rose glasses
Can't teach you tomorrow
If you're dragging
Yesterday

Dead City Rot
Dead City Rot
The time is coming
When green laughing flower
Will dance on your grave

The goal will be
For those that proceed

On the top of
Your rotten dead corpse
Disintegrating
Underneath fresh flesh thoughts

To feverishly discontinue
Everything you stood for
Everything that you taught

DEAD CITY
DEAD CITY ROT

MOTHER NATURE HATES US

After we killed her baby
A mother elephant
Terrorized a village night after night
When we finally killed her
We discovered
She had eaten human flesh
An herbivore ate meat
Thus,
Do you know how much hate
She had to have for us?

Mother Nature hates us

Tourist smashed and ate a hexapus
The second one ever discovered
You can bet that Mother Nature hates us

Beached whales
Beached porpoises
Beached dolphins too
Mother Nature hates us all
Even you

The rainforest is still burning

Heatwave
Heatwave
Go find some water
Heatwave
Heatwave
Sacrifice a daughter

Chemical runoff
Runs with the pack
A simple humanitarian hack

Dead fish dead birds
Dead birds dead fish
When they're all gone
You get a free wish

When the sea levels rise
It's only a momentary demise
At least in the planet's eyes

Another oil spill
More contaminated water
Do I sound ungrateful?
As we head to the slaughter

Mother Nature hates us

Poison ivy loves climate change
If I could only scratch
This rash on my brain

Will your city disappear?
It's in God's hands so have no fear
And if it does
Our thoughts and prayers
Go out to everyone

Island of garbage
The new paradise
The view is the same
And you can't beat the price

Waves of trash
Shaken and stirred
With expensive
Pharmacological turds

Oil slick spreads
As clean-up continues
On the next episode of
The Earthling's Blues

Who's profiting off our descent?
Maybe the private corporate government

Hurricanes, floods, and electrical storms
Tornadoes and fires we call them the norm

Mother Nature hates us

When you're there you don't have to look far
The Baobab trees are not the only things
Going extinct in Madagascar

Rhino meet the Dodo
You're basically the same
When it comes to how
We play the game

Now animals hunt us
Just to kill
The Animal Kingdom's
Evolutionary thrill

The rainforest is still burning
Village under siege
Attack of the jungle monkey
Evolution my friend
You're a twisted junkie

Drought
Drought
Try and dig ourselves out
Drought
Drought
Balancing hope and doubt

The rainforest is still burning

Destruction of the forests
And ancient rock formations
But leave the statues of our idols up
Because we're such a proud nation

Ragweed pollen
Mass death of bees
Are we sure we're killing off
The correct species?

Mother Nature hates us
Mother Nature hates us

The rainforest is still burning

After we killed her baby
A mother elephant
Terrorized a village night after night
When we finally killed her
We discovered

She had eaten human flesh
An herbivore ate meat
Thus,
Do you know how much hate
She had to have for us?

CLICK-BAIT HAIKU

A.

There's only one left

Just act now to make it yours

Take the life from it

OUR DEFAUNATION FETISH

Look here, young blood
This used to be our planet
It had many evolutions
Before we humans ran it

There were also extinctions
That killed off most everything
So back to evolution
For the remaining species

Over some time
Species evolved
Even with territorial predators
They thrived and survived

Dinosaurs at one time
Were at the top of the food chain
Before an asteroid came
And killed everything

Once again species slowly evolved
After the previous era's creatures dissolved

Birds and mammals
Insects and fishies
There are so very many
Or at least there used to be

Nobody complained
When the bramble cay melomys went away
Get rid of all rats most people did say

Then there's the passenger pigeon
The cheap food in the sky
They gobbled all up
Till no more did fly

They hunt, ate, destroyed
Or caged
Every living creature
With an unsympathetic rage

Gold, black, grizzly and polar bears
Just fairy tale creatures, but once they were real

Baiji white fin dolphin was the first to go
Like the Javan, Sumatran, African Black
And the White Rhinos

Butterflies butterflies and so many birds
I read the auk, the dodo, the parakeets,
The Spix's Macaw and ivory-billed woodpecker
All sounded extremely cool

Critical habitats
Consumed for consumption
Demise being the obvious presumption

Invertebrates 97% of all species
Gone all gone like the fishies
Amphibians had the best run
They survived all extinctions
Except that last one

I really loved the Pinta Island tortoise
The magical world they must have enjoyed
Before all of us

The ibex, oryx, antelope and deer
If it had horns, it has disappeared
The Tasmanian and Javan tigers didn't last very long
Lions lasted the longest
A true king's swan song

I wonder if the marine mammals
Felt sorry for us
Or did they just consider humans
Treasonous

Before the last elephant collapsed
The woolly mammoth was the largest mammal around
They killed them both off
Which is such a let down

Poaching, poisoning, loss of food, habitat destruction and
just
plain Greed
By our foolish family tree
A pattern continued by generations of us
The earth's conscious virus

We thought the End Permian was bad!
Humans destroyed more than
An asteroid had

When our ancestors cared more about
Money and machine guns
Yes, welcome to The Holocene Event
A human function
The Anthropocene culture Super Predator
Of the Sixth Mass Extinction

Now young blood, learn from our ancestors past
Don't make the mistakes that they had made
Create a sustainable organization

Because there's no reason to rush into
The next planetary extinction

KITCHEN NIGHTMARE

A dirty fan should always be the first indication
Time is irrelevant
Or at the very least
Impertinent

A clean kitchen
Is the ass
You want to eat off of

In the kitchen an ass
Is something you serve sauced up

My grandmother on my mother's side
Died
Before I could meet her
But it was said she drank beer
In and out of
The kitchen

My father's mother
Made my favorite lemon cake
Verna was her name
She had the softest skin
And an alcoholic's shake

I couldn't imagine
I would never assume
That all the food that I eat
I shouldn't consume

Your grandparents
And your parents' grandparents before
Their grandparents
And theirs before

Cleaned to survive
Cleaned and served good food
They all got us this far, so be sure
If the fans are nasty
You'll cook for your own

DRIED HUMAN HEARTS
& STUFFED HUMAN SOULS

Thoughts are packaged and sold
Like frozen food

Consistent precipitation of acid rain
In the belly of our personal ocean
Bought by the cart full

Who remembers
Watching the planted seed
As it slowly blooms
Under a guiding sun
Developing anticipation
For an immediate but timely
Harvestation

Then using all the right spices
Creating an aroma
That makes your palms perspire

Butterflies flutter for freedom
Your mouth moistens like the end of winter

Placed gently into the fire
Only to be pulled
At just the right moment
Knowing that every drip
Will be licked without waste
And felt throughout the body

You create thoughts
You don't reheat them

KBEARE'S LITTLE HELPER

If this shovel is in your hands

Your night has taken an unfortunate turn

For you'll be digging a hole for Kbeare

From which you may not return

Love is a deep pit

I'M NO FAN OF DRIVING

It's a beautiful day in the morning
The perfect time for a walk
Hello how are you my neighbor
Oh, how the birds sing and talk

Here is my pod of evil
My four-wheel drive pod of evil
Sitting in my pod of evil
Hating you all the same

I love riding my bike
On a bright and sunny day
It's also fun in a drizzle
Just be sure to practice safety

Here in my pod of evil
I'm a racist intolerant prick
Here in my pod of evil
Road-rage is making me sick

It's a beautiful evening for a wonderful walk
And a wonderful walk we shall have
Mmmm…Ahhhh…Doesn't it feel good
To stretch out those really tight calves?

Here in my pod of evil
My heart's about to explode
Here in my pod of evil
Everyone off the road

I love it so much when I'm out and about
When I'm not
When I'm not
Stuck in my pod of evil

FASHION FLAMBÉ

Only a fool feels fashion forward
For every fashionista
A fairy finds its fatality

Being fashion fresh
Has nothing to do with
The latest trends

Only a fool feels fashion feels good
Fashion hurts
Like fire forever feverishly flourishing
Deep within your skin
Cutting off vital blood
Gripping you from within

Only a fool follows fashion fads
Corporate cons constructing their funds
From foolish fashion followers
Emotional exploitation FOR EVERYONE

Looking luxurious with confidence
A fabulous fleeting fashion sensation

Dressed to impress
Forever fashionably depressed

CLICK-BAIT LUNE

A.

Merciless death air

Fires raged hard

We were forced to leave

FUMBLING IN THE DARK

Supplements and lubricants
Bone density exercises
I'm told
Are the best defense

Compacted lower back bills
Silent calls from surviving children
Moving is next to impossible
Yet tragedy shortens the distance

I can barely catch my breath
In my black & white dreams
I'm sure color
would certainly kill me

I know how you feel
As you're losing feeling
It hurts to laugh
Like a good friend leaving

I found my bliss
In my brain's dark tiki soundtrack trip
There the cocktails are strong
So only consume a few sips

Let me sleep in
Until you miss me
I'm right here
Trying to melt away quietly

Take another deep breath
And relax your brow gently
Wishes are free
Which you can drown in slowly

I can't open my third eye
I'm blind in this hive
Fumbling my way through
Reminding myself to survive

WOULD YOU KILL ME?

I agree with you
I can tell how you feel
And by the look of your face
You haven't taken your pill

Nor have I
Because I'm hoping you'll stay
If you truly love me
Then I'm better
I'm better this way

I know
And you don't need to mention
That this whole conversation
Is the only part of your dissension

I understand it's not you
Fulfilling this frustration
It's the thought of me
Not being a potential

At this point would you say
I'm better off
Not living this way?

If I agree with you
That gives the okay

So my question is
Would you kill me today?

SO CLOSE

Put it
So close to the heart
Put it
So close to the brain
Put it
So close to the mainframe
Put it
In your mouth
Put it
At the beginning
Put it
At the end
Put it where they can see
Put it so they can't see
Put it
In everything that's gone wrong

Put it away
None of it is worth it
Not then
Not today

So Close

THE EMPTINESS

The road trip has gone off the cliff

Expectations are now extinct

The garden dried up

The computer crashed

The virus is incurable

The bullet unreachable

And the doctor is nowhere to be found

The stars flickered out

The song is no longer heard

The storm has taken everything

The emptiness

Fills the glass I drink from

DARK SPIRITS

It took some serious thought
But when I think about it
It is
The Spirits that haunt

When you find yourself
Waking up
With a gun to your head
The question you will obviously ask is
What did I did?

I
Prefer to think
And I hope you concur
That I saved the day

(Obviously not for me
But someone worthy)

And thus this bullet
Wasn't specifically for me

Then
I realize
The gun to my head
Which, now in my mouth
Is just a sad story
I'm thinking about
That my subconscious brought

That constantly
Rotates
In my waking thoughts

I wish my hangovers
Caused pain
Like they did
When I was young and drinking

Katzenjammer mornings
Are not
For me

Dark Spirits
In my simple machine

A FUNNY THING ABOUT PAIN

It's funny
When they say
That your suffering
Makes you who you are today

Like a scar you've hidden
that when discovered
Is considered
A sexy part of your
Character

I say funny
As if
Your insurance check
Came in

And they paid you what you thought you would get
With a solid eccentric, extravagant bonus check

And a handwritten company card
That says "Sorry we fucked up"
Here's your reward

Funny cause you might have
Lost a limb
Or a kid
Or your brain or a pet
But a hand written card
And a bonus check
Might make you smile
Just for a sec

It's funny cause you know
If we don't laugh
We will blow

It matters
Your pain
Eventually
We all feel the same

And it pains me to say
I feel your despair
Smiling on the inside
Well, we've made it to here

ODE TO WILLIAM S. BURROUGHS

Pick your poison wisely

We should have realized as the words fell from your mouth like ashes only to be reformed back into tobacco and smoke themselves.

Like a caged Hopi Shaman predicting the unavoidable destruction of current and forthcoming generations, your stories carry the weight of a million slaughtered buffalo.

Nevertheless, we foolishly ignored it. But you knew this about us and proceeded to live in the stench of our dying and decaying society. Much like a vulture who lives in shame but committed to cleaning up what we've left behind.

We can't all live to be ancient, or an elder, and only a small batch of us will have the future to be wise. I know this pains some people to hear, but by God, it's the truth and we all must accept it.

You warned us it would get worse and holy hell it has detonated. It's as if the bastards have always had a plan to exterminate most of us. Not that we've needed a nudge to find ourselves in unfortunate experiences, but that hasn't stopped them from catapulting us into the fire with purpose.

So your words that echo in the dry canyons of our minds should be a reminder to let bygones be bygones because soon enough we too shall be gone.

If you find yourself in Heaven and happen to run into
my son
Buy him a drink, or whatever poison he's chosen.

PERFECT SENSE

When you can hear yourself
And it's a different being
When you wake up and realize
You don't know what you're seeing

When the call comes in
When the silence has words
Like a deafening quake
Forever disturbed

The right word
The wrong choice
The right trigger
The wrong noise

Nervous reactions
Without control
Just remorse

Anxiety feels like forever trying to park
Can I get silence please, and a landmark?

Arriving is a must

The uninvited rest of us
Must volunteer and adjust

Now looking back I can say
It makes
Perfect sense
For us to be this way

HIT OR MISS, CHAMP

The hardest part
Isn't when it hits

The hardest part
Is the subconscious
Steering the unconscious

The car
Out of control
Before the collision

The pain rests
Between the action
And the conclusion

It's only conversation
It's only belligerent
Distraction

Death is
The hardest
Unconscious
Conclusion

Belligerent breath
Is
And will always be
The car
Before the collision

I will see you
Every time
I drive
Into
A
Conversation

CLICK BAIT SENRYU

A.

I worry so much

Then remember that

I raised you with love

B.

I love you deeply

And when I hear your sweet voice

I feel so lucky

CLICK BAIT LUNE

B.

When the big one hits

Out of state

I sure hope to be

C.

Alone so alone

Floating off

Into nothingness

FESTIVAL FRIENDS

I love how we bond
On the drive to the event
It's as if our friendship
The Universe had sent

A collection of likes
With an acknowledging nod
I understand what you're saying
Without listening at all

I can be invaluable
If I like the story in your pitch
The soft ego is delicate
Of a deceitful sellout snitch

Slurping and chirping
A flipping bird citizen
Focused on acting like
A selfish hedonist in the end

Don't let your attraction
Be why you stay
Outside of your smile
It's the fastest to fade

It's the name of the game
And that's how we win
Said no one
Over eight years
On their deathbed

Now I'm wandering around
Alone and discontent
The group I was with
Dissolved in resent

I realize now each moment is fleeting
It's never about forever
It's only about meeting

A silent ride home
I was a fool not to see
Festival friends
Are all we seem to be

CLICK BAIT SENRYU

C.

OMG!!

The fucking injustice… have you heard?

Devastating!

D.

What-ifs are just myths

We tell ourselves to feed

The head with ghostly guilt

E.

Once they reach a certain age

Failed suicidals with suicidal tendencies

Figure there's no need

F.

Like the sore feeling of over masturbating

Or freezing your brain from ice cream overeating

The numbness is pleasantly excruciating

MY CRIPPLING ADDICTION

I'm a pacifist
I'm a pacifist
Peace, Love, Unity, Harmony
I have to focus on this

I have a debilitating
And crippling addiction
It's haunted me since
I was just a little one

I know it's there
I try not to give in
But before I realize
There it is

When you have an addiction
It's like having a friend
That gives you some love
Except when you need it

I do understand
Addictions so well
It's a teacher and a lover and
A comfortable hell

And like teachers and lovers
We have so many in life
But the one I can't shake
That causes the most strife

This teacher
This lover
The worst addiction
I have…

Well, before I go on
I want to make sure you understand
Addictions are deeper
Than what's in each hand

Not all addicts
Lose control
Most addicts hide it
Deep in their soul

That addiction I can't shake
Is the feeling of
Controllable hate
Getting frustrated and angry
Is an addictive fate

I won't give you details
This is all I will tell
So that I can focus on being
Emotionally well

If you're like me
This you should know
Addictions can be controlled
Because if that weren't the case...

I'm a pacifist
I'm a pacifist
Peace, Love, Unity, Harmony
I just keep meditating on this

I HATE TODAY
SO I SHOULD SAY THIS

It's hard to breathe at this depth
When you're gasping for the smallest breath
When your last thought is your thought
Accepting death

I wake up under water
My only breath is my last
When I give up and give in
My eyes grasp the past

It is you!
I should have said
Because it was you that did
Breathe life back into
This balloon of a head

I really don't know
How I consistently submerge
Under so much pain
Until you emerge

Like today
Like before
Like what I know will come

I would die under it all
Without you
I am drowned

I hate today
But I should say

Without you I am just air
Hoping to be

Something more than just stuck
Deep in this sea

I'M TO BLAME

At the end of the day
There's no shying away
I guess you could say
That I'm to blame

I never thought it would end
Quite like this
I never wanted to see your eyes
So dark and so pissed

It was never my intentions
It was not planned out
But I can tell by your look
You have serious doubts

Even if it wasn't me
It's something I would do
So once it happened
I knew I would be blamed by you

When patterns are created
When the character sticks
When it's right on par
If the shoe fits

It doesn't need to be correct
For you to feel stronger
So I'll take the fall
Don't look any longer

At the end of the day
There's no shying away
I guess you could say
That I'm to blame

CLICK-BAIT SENRYU

G.

Fuck you fuck you, do

Go fuck yourself gently

Till your face turns blue

YOU LOOKING AT ME?

Let me start off by saying
It's never my intent
To do you, or anyone
Any harm, that is
Unless…

I think you deserve
A poke or a prod
Or a verbal stick
In your proverbial
Fraud

It's not that I'm looking
To feel angry inside
About what you did or said
And how it affected my mind

But sometimes it comes off
Like you're looking for a fight
And when I look in your eyes
I think I just might…

Now look where we are
This is no fun at all
Thinking this way
Will be our downfall

So you go your own way
And I shall go mine
And the next time we meet
May our moods be benign

CLICK-BAIT SENRYU

H.

Disagreeing words

If only to be a dick

Argumentative

I'M A NICE PERSON

CONDESCENDING

BELITTLING

PATRONIZING

DEMEANING

FIGHT PICKING

THOUGHT POKING

PUSHING IT

SARCASTIC DICK

FUCKING WITH

AND

STARTING SHIT

Ask yourself
Am I doing any of this?

I'LL TAKE THE TIME

I was just going to start this
But thought it would be better
If I took the time
To let you know
I'll take the time
Thought maybe I should
Stop doing what I'm doing
Because it wasn't
What I needed to be doing
Nor what I even started out doing

So resetting, restarting
Rebuilding beginning
So that I can say that
What I'm doing
Is taking time
To consider the thought
Of taking the time
The time that you mentioned
Because in the time that we've missed
With this consideration
Has consumed
All the time
The time that I have
And time as you know
Is something I'm very considerate on
And I'll take the time
To consider a better method
Of taking my time

ODE TO WINONA LADUKE

Oh wise First Daughter
Oh great and mighty Earth Sister
Protector of Water
You are the spirit that thunders
Voice of those unheard
I honor you

Bring us together on the basis of respect
In the time of the Seventh Fire
Guide us on the right path
Lead us to the Eighth Fire
A green path
With less stuff
And more love

We shall follow we shall lead
Re-envision Re-create
Grow hemp and hope in our gardens
Indigenous Earthling
Medicine Makers
Fighting for environmental justice
We shall be the sustainable solution
For a new era of evolution

Oh wise First Daughter
Oh great and mighty Earth Sister
Protector of Water
You are the spirit that thunders
Voice of those unheard
I honor you

YOU DON'T BELIEVE IN MAGIC

I'm a manifester
My dreams I like to create
For if it wasn't for manifesting
My life I would surely hate

Manifesting is how you make magic
And magic is how you manifest
If you practice often
Quite good, you shall get

Now here's where the magic begins
And it's no sleight of hand
Magic is manifesting
To create what you have planned

First I dream a dream
It's as easy as it seems
It's best, starting off
Not to make it too extreme

I'm a manifester
So the second thing I do
Is stew on all the ways
To make my dreams come true

Then I follow through
Which is no easy feat
But once you've manifested
Then your magic is complete

I'm a manifester
I make my dreams come alive
I do it all with magic
So that my thoughts will thrive

You don't believe in magic
Well, if that works for you
I guess that you could say
You're a manifester, too

YOUR MOMMA

Your Momma
Your Momma
Your Momma's drinking wheatgrass
I've seen her in the morning with a big tall green glass
She's growing it up like the Gaia Earth Mother
She's drinking it down like I've seen no other

Your Momma
Your Momma
Your Momma's eating tons of kale
Dehydrated chips and fresh salads by the bale
She's growing it up like the Gaia Earth Mother
She's chewing it down like I've seen no other

Your Momma
Your Momma
Your Momma's growing hella weed
She says it's a strain that's rich in CBD
She's growing it up like the Gaia Earth Mother
She's burning it down like I've seen no other

Your Momma's a nut when it comes to her health
She knows deep down it's the greatest wealth
Your Momma
Your Momma
Your Pachamama

YOU'RE A ROAR

You my dear
Should be on the silver screen
Not bumping around town
With a bimbo like me

You're the bee's knees
All sweet honey and berries
A voracious bearcat symphony

You hotsy totsy
Fresh tomato
A spifflicated Sheba
Choice bit of calico

A tall glass of water
A shimmering star
With what you're working with, darling
You're destined to go far

Never a bluenose
Never a canceled stamp

Cash in a smooch on the cheek
With this zozzled tramp

You my dear
Should be on the silver screen
But I'm glad you're here
With a dewdropper like me

A HEALTHY
LOVE POEM

I've got phlegm a mile wide
And you want to kiss me tonight?
My body stinks
I'm sweating glue
And my sticky tar mouth
Wants to kiss you too

Parasites
In your eyes
I see what's on the inside

Bacteria
Infested veins
I need ants in my blood
To keep me clean

My nervous system
Is SHOT
Your touch feels like an electric shock

Rash on my skin
From using detergent
Even bleeding out
The situation's never urgent

The air is diseased
Just like the sea
So it seems like a good time
To start our recovery

We all have needs
Consciously
I hope you choose
What works for me

Just be like me
But only what you perceive
Our excuses excusing every brutality

Why are we so socially sadistic?
Yet personally masochistic

Superficial fantasy sensation
I'm just peering in
From another dimension

Don't forget to breathe
When
Anxious tendencies
Remove the ease of relaxation

Pale skin
Almost translucent
I'm alright, just slightly wounded

Are you okay?
Should I refrain
From pointing out
The misleading?

Separate the body
From the mind
I think I'll try not to think tonight

I wish I could heal
All my free-radical damage
My body is a temple
And in it lives a savage

If I were sick
And somewhat insane
Would you still love me the same?

A SUSTAINABLE
LOVE POEM

Pattern of communication
Pattern of understanding
Pattern of supporting
Pattern of sharing

Pattern is form from the pressure
We apply from each side
Creating our love design

Our energy flows
Surging out in all directions
Spiraling from the center
Finding loving zones and sectors

Tight spirals and lobes
Moments we identify
Opposite spirals make a blossom
Unexpected momentary surprise

Our sweet summation series
Branching patterns of development
Splintering again and again
Every look in your eyes is a new ascent

Netting together strengthening links
Our love snowflake
Held together with tension
Of give and take

Give and take looks random
But is exactly precise
We're an off-centered sphere
An infinite love vice

In our garden of patterns
My love for you grows
As we live every day
Supporting our flow

SQUEEZES

I give you all my squeezes
And all my smirks
All my smiles
They're just some of my perks

I give you all my deep breaths
And all my sighs
All my stares
There's just you and I

I give you all my assurance
And all my faith
All my trust
There's just us and space

Pull me close
And together we ride
We're just about to hit our stride

I give you all my dreams
And all my nights
All my love
Squeezes of delight

CLICK BAIT SENRYU

I.

Her sweet smile reveals

A dark pain within her soul

I know how she feels

J.

Your touch like warm cream

Soothes my nervous skin

Safe again it says

K.

Sunrise at our spot

Cool moon air warm sunlight

Your hand my soft kiss

CLICK BAIT LUNE

E.

Slow meditation

With dry palms

On hot desert nights

F.

We hunt for cool air

Desire

Splendor in the breeze

DOWN TO THE GRAVY

The pinto beans are soaking
There's a quarter of a bag of rice
A can of green beans or corn
The wrapper's come off
So it's your guess or mine

The chips and the salsa were the first things to go
Now I'm down to Tabasco and an overripe tomato

Plenty of salted crackers
And a box of powdered pancakes
I could do a little fishing
But hell, there's no clean lakes

Tortillas with butter
All out of freshwater

Barbeque, soy, and Worcestershire sauce
A container of bad goulash

Some mayonnaise in a jar
An empty mustard bottle
One old egg I won't eat
A hundred pennies make a dollar

Some chicken in the freezer
Last Thursday I had for dinner
There's three beers in the refrigerator
I think I'll have for lunch

THESE NUTS

They started out as a snack
But they've become the main meal
I'm having a hard time stopping
The way that I feel

I need to be patient
When handling a few
Some nuts are hard to crack
Symbolically blue

A good solid nut
Takes work to get
I hope you're good with your hands
And ready to sweat

Don't be ashamed
If you need to use tools
Use everything you have
To reach that sweet jewel

I could talk for days on the subject
I'm not allergic in any way
Nuts and I go back
A very long way

Peanut of course was my gateway to
The richness of almond and the sweet cashew

Hazelnut
You know you're fine
But mixed with chocolate
You're absolutely divine

I like my nutty lovers just a bit toasted
Like those crazy Chestnuts and macadamias
Are best when they're roasted

Pistachio
You elegant high class ho
If only
I could afford you

Like your nutty mistress friends
The pine nut and Brazilian
To nibble on all of you
I'd put the work in

Sunflower and sesame you freaks
You're just seeds
But I'm down to get freaky
If you want to nut butter for me

The creamy the crunchy
The chunky and the buttery
I'm so happy I'm not allergic
To this rich savory sluttery

THE SUN WILL COME OUT TOMORROW

Can't find anything on TV tonight
Maybe tomorrow

Sit here reading this magazine
Got all these things I need to do
Can't think of one of them right now
Could call my partner up and tell them I love them
Maybe tomorrow

I'll just sit back and let the music fill my head
Like warm bath water
I should take a shower
Maybe tomorrow

Drink myself to sleep tonight
Go to work in the morning
I keep looking at myself in the mirror
Such a simple thing to do
Find myself another option
Maybe tomorrow

Take a walk
Eat some food
Chase my dreams around the room
Could head over to visit you
Try and convince each other we always knew
Maybe tomorrow

Still nothing on TV
Is the world alive outside?
I guess I'll find out tomorrow

THE SKY IS FALLING, GIVE ME A MINUTE

I just heard
We're so fucked!
How long do we have
Till the asteroid has sunk?

All the things I don't need
To worry about anymore
The payments I didn't make
The repairs to the car

Oh what a relief
Now I don't have to go
To that expo
In Vegas
With that "employee"
You know…

Now we're oddly free
And I might feel better if I tell
It was me who ran up your bar bill
And well...

I'm also thankful
That now I can finally say
Where your good booze
And your drugs went away

It was me that day
It was also me... that day

I also forgive you
For your lies and deceit
Did I mention that I
Had sex with your partner's feet

None of it matters
We're now instantly myth
I hope that this little conversation
Hasn't left you piss-miffed

Now that the air is clear
Well, almost, almost
I forgot to mention
And this isn't
A boast

It's also no big deal
So, no need to trip
You should know now
Because of this asteroid shit

But when your mom was in town
You know, after the divorce…

Look we're fucked
This we know
So how long do we have
Till the asteroid...OHHH!

MR. GARBAGE MAN

Mr. Garbage Man what do you see
Bits and pieces of a sick society?

Mr. Garbage Man do you hear
The sound of a people living in fear?

Mr. Garbage Man do you think
Have we pushed our culture to the brink?

Mr. Garbage Man can you tell
That as a species if we have failed?

Mr. Garbage Man do you know
If we will reap what we sow?

Mr. Garbage Man I want to thank you
We're always making messes
And you're always coming through

FREE GAME

Your happy holy vice
Is lazy larping
While you work
You're just whistle-blowing

In your personal virtual fantasy
A comic convenience
Of soft-core
Skinny dipping sauce

In your future I see
Physical street art therapy
In the comfortable setting of
Your colored light dependency

HOW TO LOSE
CONSCIOUSNESS IN A DREAM

Dada crack

Snap back

Thought sap

Forward trap

Abstract palette

Sap trap

Back snap

Palate crack

Forward thought

Dada abstract

YOU WERE
SAYING SOMETHING?

I don't know
Where to begin
Where did I leave off?
Or did I just end?

In disbelief
Confused on sight
To tell the tale
As it wanders
Through the dark desert at night

It orbits
But never lands
Like a deaf man
Without hands

Where are we going?
Have we been here before?
This is not what I thought
Did you knock on the door?

Misplaced words
Like the keys to the car
With a handful of words
I mumble-
I don't need to go far

Huh?
What?
What is it that you said?
Let's talk about a friend of a friend

Would I say
If you weren't here?
That slipped out
So pretend you didn't hear

Speak up if you will
And try and make yourself clear

I dropped it
You caught it
So go ahead and take it home

I'm lost
But at least I'm not alone

Did that just make sense?
Did you comprehend?

Or am I talking
In a foreign language again?

IT'S IN MY DNA

I was seven
When my parents divorced
We moved in with my mom's sister and her husband
He worked for the Navy
And they lived next to the base
I remember the first night we arrived
In the hot high desert air
We swam in their cool pool
Looking to the sky smothered with stars
I said "A UFO!"
My aunt muttered, "It's a plane.
I guess he doesn't know."
But
I knew, I knew, I always knew

Throughout my school years
My friends were the outcasts
The geeks, the punks, the weirdos
The ones that also believed
We weren't alone in the galaxy
The ones that knew
And that knew
I knew, I always knew

In my twenties
We would meet in the back of pizza restaurants
Passing around and watching
Through the fuzzy, blacked-out scattered information

Outdated transmissions
From photocopies and VHS tapes
We had accumulated
I knew, I always knew

In my thirties
I studied under Zecharia Sitchin
Read Erich Von Daniken
I never doubted the Hills
And Bob Lazar never sounded bizarre
Because
I knew, I always knew

Now In my late forties
Our government finally admits
There's technology that is far beyond ours
Out there, in the air, in the sea
Maneuvering in directions and speeds
Far beyond what we can achieve
And all I can say is
I knew, I always knew

I might not see it in my life
But it will be in an historical blink of an eye
When the religious companies
And world governments all agree
(It's been known for centuries)
That they're here and have been
That we know where they're from
How they got here
Why they're here
And if we'll be overrun

Then everyone will say
I knew, I always knew

REPTOIDS

Poison all water
And charge us to
Drink
With dehydration
It's hard to
Think

Fattening us up
With sugary
Treats
With malnutrition
We're easily
Beat

Gradually
Firing up
The pot
Turn our planet
Into a desert
They like it
Hot!

Destroy our dreams
So effectively
They don't dream
So neither
Should we

Deplete
ALL
Water
It's not
Our right
To drink

De-hy-drated...
Hard
To
Think

Hypnotized
Into
Defeat
Soon to be
The species
They
Eat

ODE TO AMY GOODMAN

When asked, "Where do you get your news?" Without missing a beat, I say I start my mornings with Amy Goodman, every weekday. She first caught my ear in the mid-1990s and I was immediately enamored. I was ripe and ready to receive her daily updates from the subversive movement. An activist in my midtwenties with a goal of bettering the world and a desire to educate the brainwashed masses; whether or not they wanted an education- I was determined! As civilizations rise and fall, Amy Goodman has been there, reporting the situations often in horrific detail, breaking through the illusion to wake up the brainwashed masses. I heard her and still do. In war and peace, her voice cries out, "THIS WAY!" and I run head-on in Amy Goodman's direction.

Amy Goodman is an anthropologist at heart, and by degree. Determined to create social responsibility. Reporting on the drilling and killing, violence against indigenous people, their culture, water and land, from the greedy corporations and politicians. Amy Goodman makes entire countries nervous about the truths she might expose. She's been shot at, beaten, and arrested so that the truth we shall know. A frontline reporter, detained and distressed, looks like Amy Goodman has another warrant for her arrest. Not a corn dog editorialist, Amy Goodman is a fact-based investigative journalist. Always hostile and combative to Injustice and those that impose it.

All the prizes and awards in the world wouldn't be enough to honor the job you do daily, for us.

Amy Goodman, you are the voice of our silenced majority.

MY MOMMA

My momma always said
I love you
Now go wash your face and brush your teeth
Cut your fingernails and always have clean hands
Sleep tight and I'll see you in the morning

My momma always said
Be safe, it's not you I don't trust, it's everyone else
You can't choose your family, but you can choose
To avoid them
If the friends you choose do stupid shit
You're bound to be stupid with them

My momma always said
Respect women, be gentle, kind and understanding
Never let the romance die
Remember the little things
Always laugh if given the chance

My momma always said
Do what you love and the money will follow
The beauty is in the journey so journey often
Art is just glue and popsicle sticks
Life is just glue and popsicle sticks
Be good and create with love

My momma

YOUR KIDS SHOULD KNOW

Your kids should know

Your great grandma danced in the park
High on LSD
Your great grandpa smoked weed
And loved mushroom tea

Your kids should know
Your grandpa has his years
Of plowing through snow
Spent a good deal of money
Packing his nose
Your grandma was more of a
Goofball girl
Nurses don't fear needles
And she was a nurse on the go

Your kids should know

Your mother raved on MDMA
Not just one dose
And not just one day
Your father just smoked some pot
Which he grew outside
And well, maybe he emptied a million or so
Cartridges of nitrous oxide

But that shouldn't come as a surprise
Your great-great grandpa huffed ether
And nitrous with some dentist geezer
And your great-great-great grandmother
Smoked reefer with jazz musicians behind the theater

You should tell your kids

You should talk about drugs
And the fun that you had
As well as the times
You were miserable and sad

The dangers and side effects
And all the great sex
That they could have
As drugs are complex

Because hypocrisy is a veil
That's covered in shit
And we know who you really are
When hiding behind it

You should tell your kids
You should talk about drugs

But what do I know?
It's all for you to decide
It's your family show

But don't you think
Your kids should know?

THERE ONCE WAS A MAN WHO SOLD MUSHROOMS

There once was a man who sold mushrooms
He sold them high and low
His advice was always to start
With a small dose that he calls micro

There once was a man who took mushrooms
He felt the more he ate would be great
So he gobbled them up
Then after the ounce he threw up
Spent days in a five dimensional debate

There once was a lady who took mushrooms
She made it into a tea
After a cup and a half
She just giggled and laughed
Then gave me her secret recipe

You can always take more
But you can never take less
A lesson best understood
Yet so many must test

There are some minds
That need to blow
To find what they need
Some dose macro

For this path if you choose
Your ego you shall lose

But fear not my friend
For your journey will not end
With you just babbling into the universe

Your guide is a pro
So just take it slow
Relax and forego
And just let it all flow

Remember
You won't be like this forever

There once was a man who sold mushrooms
They say he's a super fun guy
He suggests that your dose is micro
Unless your ego you need to die

ODE TO TERENCE MCKENNA

The language of

What is going on
What is going on?

Rock collecting
Butterflies
Weird naturalism
I Ching
Cannabis consciousness

Five dried grams
Psychonaut
Technology shaman
Head first
Freak culture
Mystic mumbo jumbo

High rapping conversations

Entity encountering experiences
Machine elves from hyperspace
Dimensional aliens
Intelligent entities
Bats in the belfry

Activism and orgies
Anti Establishment
Apocalyptic jungle

The other
The presence
Invisible landscapes
Illuminated true hallucinations

Interconnected
Labyrinths

Alien Beauty
Alien intent
Novelty producing illusion
Complexity comlexification

Time's speeding up
More events
Stuff going on
More and more
Happening

The universe is getting its act together
Through connectivity

Riding the time wave
Reaching for
The omega point
Within the cosmic giggle

DIVINE PLEASURES

I want to take you
Come with me
To meet the almighty
And float with the stars in Heaven

I want to take you
Come with me
To meet the almighty
And dance through the halls of Valhalla

I want to take you
Come with me
To meet the almighty
And swim through the rivers of Nirvana

I want to take you to the highest heights
I want to bathe you in vibrant visualizations
I want to remind you there's meaning
Through full body sensations

Come with me
Get high with me

And let us dine in the divine pleasures

MAKING GIGGLE BUTTER

Giggle Therapeutics was my cannabis company name, and Giggle Butter, the product we produced, was deliciously insane. I first made it for my wife, who didn't like to smoke. Having never really done it, the smoke made her choke. But when she came home at night from roller derby she was always wound-up and beat-up. Unable to sleep until it was almost time to get up. So I infused some coconut oil and it was quickly her favorite way to consume a little cannabis at the end of her long day.

Long ago I learned a method, a way to make edibles taste, just like the food you're cooking and not an ashtray. So an infused dinner was eaten, every magical bit. And as soon as my wife started giggling... I knew we had a hit.

The giggle guided us up and down California, demo-ing and giggle-spreading. We met a shit ton of con artists and a few people we call family.

We were lucky enough to get out before the greedy corporate
buy out.

Now I bring it back around, to the old school home brew just for you. Now you too can make giggle butter at home just like I do.

In fact, I think everyone and their mother should all know how to make delicious cannabis products whether they simmer or they bake. So let us begin, let's start the class, what it all starts with is washing your grass.

Simmer, Simmer, Simmer makes the cannabis plant taste thinner. Less cannabis taste, the more you can taste your dinner. Or breakfast, or brunch, or supper or lunch.

Simmer then strain then do the same. This washes your plant so you don't have to consume, everything that is on it and everything used to make it bloom.

- Weigh out ½ lb of leaf into a mesh brew bag
- Boil water in a large pot then turn it off
- Submerge bag of leaf into hot water and let sit for 45 min. to an hour
- Remove from hot water
- Squeeze out the water from bag
- Rinse bag with warm tap water until runoff is no longer green or brown

Now you're ready for decarb, decarboxylation. It's an important part, so pay close attention. If you over do it, your potency is decreased, but if you don't do it enough, on bacteria you could feast.

- Spread leaf out onto baking trays
  (Thin layers dry the quickest way)
- Bake in the oven at 245F or less until dry
  (Watch and don't over bake to crispy fry)
- Once dry pull out and let cool

Good news for you, you're almost through! You now have the main product to go be infused. Coconut oil is what we use for a base, but any fat-soluble product could be used in its place.

- ½ lb / 227g Decarbed leaf
- 6 lbs / 2724g Coconut oil
- 1 ½ lbs / 681g MCT oil

Place the leaf into a mesh bag, double if you can. Heat oils in a large pot to a simmering temp, then dunk that bag of leaf deep within.

Simmer, don't boil, and you'll have a winner. After 45 minutes let this elixir chill, then squeeze out the bag and have at will. We sweetened one with honey and spiced another with cayenne. If you do it right, you never stop giggly-enne. Here you have it my friend, I hope you have fun, spreading the giggle to everyone.

CLICK BAIT SENRYU

L.

I'll take that

I can dispose of

Contraband

M.

I take drugs

But bring them to me

Discreetly

N.

I feel it in me

Its presence is alien

But I enjoy it

CLICK-BAIT HAIKU

B.

You are my healer

Take care of me, sacrifice

Your sticky green buds

WE'VE BEEN APPROVED

Research has shown that
Each and every one of our medicines have
A proven track record that
Distracts the patient just enough
Before performing
Exactly how they wish
That it would not
We understand that this unexpected
Embarrassment is possibly an
Emergency and you'll probably need
Necessary assistance
The good news is, and I'm
Happy to say
Efficiency is our top
Line item priority, so you're
In the best hands that
Non-essential care can provide you
Equality and your health is our
Supreme priority
For without all of you
Our portfolios would be
Offensively
Lacking in financial
Security

PAPA JOE'S WINE

Down on the farm we sit in the backyard
We listen to the birds that come from afar
We think of a time when the Chumash ran free
We dream of freedom and ecstasy
We pray the police will just let us be
And we thank our lucky stars
For our landlord's hobby

Oh Papa Joe, Oh Papa Joe
Can we have another case
Of your wine, Maestro?

"Don't drink that wine!"
I've heard some say
But I'd give my right eye
For that Chardonnay

Vinegar or Zinfandel
I've had so much at this point
I can't even tell

When I run out of beer
You know where I'll be
Drinking wine in the barn
Like some goddamn Yuppie

Oh Papa Joe, Oh Papa Joe
Can we have another case
Of your wine, Maestro?

We'll fix up the farm and we know you won't pay
But we can drink till we're blind on Cabernet

He'll drink it for breakfast
But none will he sell
When was the last time Papa Joe
That you fell?

When the sun breaks through the morning fog
He'll be out calling Sarah, his faithful dog

They come from the North
They come from the South
To pour homemade wine into their mouth

We don't drink from glasses, we drink from a cup
But the last of the bottle
Might make you throw-up

So pace yourself
Like old Papa Joe
A cup an hour and you're good to go

Oh Papa Joe, Oh Papa Joe
Can we have another case
Of your wine, Maestro?

It's been a long day
It's always half of a year
At the end of a lifetime
The point is so clear

I'll be sad when I leave
Or if the house burns down
But there comes a time
When we all must leave town

Oh Papa Joe, Oh Papa Joe
Can we have another case
Of your wine, Maestro?

FUCKIN' KLOWNS

Fuckin' Klowns
Fuckin' Klowns
I can't say it enough
Be careful trusting
Some of these
Fuckin' Klowns
Bouncing around

Take it from me
When picking klowns be choosy
Be sure to skip klowns named
Boozy Snoozy Woozy or Floozy

Now I don't want to say
That klowns on a whole
Are completely bad
That isn't my goal

I don't even mind
Which make-up they choose
And I kind of like
Their big fuckin' shoes

There are party klowns
That are fun to be around
Unlike scary klowns
Hanging out at playgrounds

Don't get me wrong
I've met many a great klown
But with hundreds if not thousands
Roaming this town

I'm warning you now
Don't let your guard down

Fuckin' Klowns
Fuckin' Klowns
I can't say it enough
Be careful trusting
Some of those
Fuckin' Klowns
Bouncing around

Now I'm off to a party
I've got klown friends in town

FROM THE SIDE OF THE ROAD

With his many moon years
He balances his weight
Between the cane in his right hand
And a wall of graffiti he leans on with his left

He watches from the side of the road

Mothers driving dreams home to sleep
Men sitting in dead cars drinking cold relaxation
Hoses being moved to feed struggling lawns
Breezes pushing misplaced trash around unwanted lots
The flickering TVs through living room windows
Working faces wiping the day's sweat on tired shirts
Children being adults
Adults forgetting they were children

The sinking sun reveals holes in hope
Highlighting anxiety
Birth and death
Dogs and birds

A nearby billboard reads:

YOU'VE GOT THIS!

CLICK-BAIT HAIKU

C.

Still waters run deep

Raging waters move boulders

Stagnant water kills

FUCK WHAT THEY SAY

They say that I'm a criminal
Because of the way I feel
Yet no one have I hurt
And nothing did I steal

They say that I'm a criminal
Who should be punished for my crime
With some minimum torture
And for the maximum time

They say that I'm a threat
A danger to society
Yet I'm not sure just how
That could possibly be

They say that I'm a threat
To all of decency
You'll notice that they say this
So indignantly

They say that I'm a criminal
And the punishment should be severe
But the truth of the matter is
Their reactions are based on racist fear

They say that I'm a criminal so I'm always on the run
You know, I believe that if they could
They would criminalize all fun

It's my right to pursue happiness
Wouldn't you agree?
Why should someone else decide
What is best for me

I say that it's my life
And I shall choose how I live
If you don't like my choices
Find your own alternative

They say that I'm a criminal
They say that I'm a threat
But I'm just a responsible hedonist
And I live with no regret

ODE TO CANDY BARR

Every chance you get

Dance

Let it be your bliss
Let it set you free

When they steal you away
When they lock you in a cage
When they force you to do unthinkable things

Every chance you get

Dance

Let it be your bliss
Let it set you free

IF YOU'RE JUST
GOING TO SIT THERE

If you're just going to sit there

If you really need the attention
If you really have something to say
If you really want to change the world
To start, there is a way

Volunteer
And
Be a mentor

If you're just going to sit there, anyway

READY

Another day

Always ready

Now finally able

The ritualistic preparation
The anticipated consumption

Arriving at the perfect level

I now hover

Reverberating
As the pleasure
Fills me in

Then

Liberated

For this moment

I feel completed

READY

For another day

CLICK-BAIT HAIKU

D.

It is all fractals

As above so below, we

Are all connected

SHWA LAYTART

The satirical dark poet, Shwa Laytart, writes deep in the witching hours and dwells in the high desert underground of Las Vegas, Nevada, with the cerebral chuckwallas, raconteur roadrunners, and twisted dust devils.

Shwa received 'Finalist in Poetry' 2020 Feathered Quill Awards for his first illustrated poetry book, 'Oh, the A**holes You'll Meet!'

Also by Shwa Laytart:
The New Modern Demonology
2027-ish
Doomed Poetry
The Gray Areas Podcast Children's Picture Book
Oh, the A**holes You'll Meet!

avantpopbooks.com/pages/shwa-laytart

Second Edition

ISBN: 9798992685442
Poetry

Cover Art by Seth Singer
Bio Photo by Sugar Laytart

Avantpop Publishing
Las Vegas, Nevada
avantpopbooks.com